If I Could Speak

MADEIA JACOBS

Table of Contents

Dedication

This book is dedicated to those individuals, both present and past, whose very existence was threatened without their consent. In spite of the challenges and conflicts of that experience, we have dared to emerge.

Experience the depictions of the pain people have shared and reflections that bind us through a journey in time with words.

"UNLESS THE LORD HAD BEEN MY HELP, MY SOUL HAD ALMOST DWELT IN SILENCE..."

PSALMS 94:17

Shattered Innocence

THOUGHTS FROM A SURVIVOR...

Dear Cousin Lee Harvey

Dear Cousin Lee Harvey,

When Mama told me we were going to the "country" in Putnam, Alabama, my heart swelled up with jubilee! I loved my grandpaw, and it was always a joy to go to his big house. He had lots of land. I couldn't wait to run and play with my family there. In the "country" we slept in big beds. The ten of us slept in threes. Of course, I slept with my sisters. I had seven brothers, two sisters, and I made ten.

The term "du-ko-lu-chee" came from my sisters and me. We would laugh and play under our house or in the yard. We would laugh ourselves to death when we caught a glimpse of one of our younger brothers "du-ko-lu-chee" while they were doing a number one. My younger brothers did not know better than to hide themselves. Other than those moments a "du-ko- lu-chee" was foreign to me. The only thing I thought a "du-ko-lu-chee" was used for was to expel a number one.

When you pulled me out of a deep sleep, I reckoned it was to fetch water. That is the only thing my young, six-year-old sleepy mind could possibly come up with. I had no idea you would try to work your "du-ko-lu-chee" inside me. We were po. We were so po that I carried biscuits and preserves to school for lunch. Nevertheless, we lived a good life. We lived a life of being kind to each other and to our neighbors. Well, at least most of us. Daddy was funny and kind, but he also had his not-so-clear.

Sometimes, daddy would come in after a drinking spree and he would wake us up, all ten of us. He would say, "Sing, motherfuckers, sing." We would begin to sing in our sleepy arrested tones, "I thank you, Jesus. I thank you, Jesus." Then, he would say, "Goddamn it, you motherfuckers are out of tune." Faithfully, we would try again. I was not a foreigner to the pain of life. I started working at the age of five. I would stand on a crate to wash dishes. That didn't bother me none. I saw how hard my mama worked and tried to make a living.

In my childlike mind, I never thought she deserved the pain she endured. She made our clothes out of burlap bags. So, when my turn came, I had the hardest time understanding that joyful night in the country that you clouded with darkness. It was compounded with pus and sores that were now on my little vagina. Sometime later in Mobile, Alabama, Mama had to take me to the doctor. You gave me syphilis. The doctor said there was no cure for it. When I was twelve, six years later, I went to Birmingham, Alabama with adults from the surrounding community. There was a clinic there sponsored by the CDC (Center for Disease Control).

I think it was the Middleton Clinic. Oh, I'm not sure of the name. So much clouded my vision by then. I was glad that the CDC called for all people with syphilis to come to that clinic. They said, "There is a cure for syphilis now called penicillin." Although I did not know the other people there from the surrounding community of Prichard, Alabama they held me and supported me just like I's family. But I wonder, Lee Harvey, in the face of plenty resources and opportunities were you starving? Surrounded by luscious fields of crops, and an abundance of food, family, and love, you felt powerless.

Could it possibly be that you knew my mama was raped at the age of 19? Mama would never tell who did it. *Was it you?* In shame, she bore that pregnancy. She hid it as she worked in grandpaw's beautiful fields. Fields of crops of everything that a family could

8

want to eat. Grandpaw had over two hundred acres of land. Unlike you, mama was not educated out of ignorance. Her parents believed in service to the community. They believed in helping the sick and those in need. So, maybe you felt that my mama's children were misfits.

The older folks in our family used to talk about you. They said you had loving and kind parents that raised you up in the church. They said that you were educated, but one would never know it. They said that you were a wild seed right from the beginning. You would kill animals for no reason. They talked about how you envied your younger brother who excelled at everything he did. They said you drank, partied, and had all kinds of women. You sinned and had no regard for the sanctity of your own life. So, how could any of us expect you to have any regard for my life? You were "bankrupt." You had, as one author puts it, "ransacked your own emotions." My family had a nickname for me. They called me Moonie. They thought I had a round face with a smile that radiated like the moonlight.

I was wondering how many "Moonies" you had infected…How many "Moonies" did you sentence to life of shame, poor self-esteem, overeating, maybe drinking, giving love and not receiving, seeking, but not finding, having but not holding, wanting and not getting?

"UNLESS THE LORD HAD BEEN MY HELP, MY SOUL HAD ALMOST DWELT IN SILENCE."

PSALMS 94:17 NIV

Signed,

Moonie

Looking for Love...

"HOPE FOR LOVE, PRAY FOR LOVE, WISH FOR LOVE, DREAM FOR LOVE...BUT DON'T PUT YOUR LIFE ON HOLD WAITING FOR LOVE."

MANDY HALE, THE SINGLE WOMAN

Fallen Angel

Her wings were clipped,

As she slipped

Into deep depression.

Caused by her most prized possession

Her obsession.

To love as instructed by the One above

The Father of love, his bride to be,

For she could not see

His infinite affection toward her direction.

She was always under His protection

Consumed by her own *infection* of *insurrection.*

I Feel Violated

Mesmerized by the thought of nothingness,

There I was captivated by your award-winning smile.

Bathed in the sunshine of your light,

Caressed by your words,

Not to mention your touch.

Not enough to know you and not enough not to know you.

How long did it take to unveil me and disarm me?

I willingly gave myself.

That's your ploy.

Little by little, day by day,

You took bits and pieces until you got to the core.

No forceful entry, no evidence, no traces…

Need I say more?

I feel like the whore that you once adored.

A lamb set out to pasture.

I feel violated.

Self-Hate Crime

I am the victim of a self-hate crime.

One of the worst kind.

Prostituting myself all the time.

He was looking for cheap labor,

I was willing to do him a favor,

That he could savor.

"Miss, you got the time?"

"Yes," I replied to the thief that comes in the night.

Disguised as an interested suitor

Who *ain't* on God's mission.

You tried to put me in a position.

I need perfect submission to run this race,

So that I might see *Him* face to face.

Lord, I am So Fragile

Lord, I am so fragile.

Surround me,

Engulf me,

With your love.

I Have Loved You

I have loved you

For so long.

I have loved you hard.

Why is it now that I have found you

And you deserted me?

Steve

You go around the church forming intimate alliances.

Taking bits and pieces of impoverished, love starved women

Who would emotionally prostitute themselves for a little piece

Of your heaven.

In the stillness of the night,

Your voice is smooth and comforting.

You welcomed me in.

I released myself.

You made me feel safe and wanted.

Over and over, I released myself.

At my most liberating moment,

You took it all in,

And then spit me out!

You Are No Different!

You hide behind your self-proclaimed piety.

You have seen your light.

You are no different from the masses of hypocrites

That have lined the church pews for centuries.

You are outraged by the injustices of this world,

But you are callous to the battles that rage within.

Oh, you sound profound,

While at the same time

Wreaking havoc to those within.

But I know your twin; he is not going to win.

You, my dear, are no different from them!

I Am A Man

Like the sanitation workers of Memphis,

All I am saying is that I am a man.

I couldn't understand what was wrong.

Somehow, I was under attack.

Unseen, I just wanted to know what my crime was?

How much time should I serve

For this undeserved treatment?

You were like a time bomb.

Every day I knew you were hurt when you were a child.

Abandoned, neglected, untrained in loving.

I read misfortune and suffering in your heart,

As your paranoia vacillated.

Between me loving you,

And you thinking you were simply a bill paver.

All I could do was offer a prayer,

As I listened to the case you built against me.

Your grandiose depiction of your food shopping

You did not shop because there was no food,

You shopped to add to the lie you would tell all over this world,

"She does not cook…"

And when you declared war on me and shouted,

"Don't cook my food either!"

I had no idea that it was all part of a plot.

A plot that had greater dimensions

Than I could see.

Oh, Liberian, Syrian…

Oh, that's right you are a Nigerian.

How your land must cry out for the inhumane crimes

You have committed against women.

Your weapon of mass destruction is your smile.

It appears warm, but it is not.

Or maybe it is your education,

Your gift of articulation.

Oh, did I mention manipulation?

You are one way in front and another way behind,

While you mastermind the kind, meek, and sincere.

You dare to smear a child of the King!

May God have mercy on you.

I wish you no harm,

For when I realized that I am a man,

And should be treated as such.

I live in symbiotic relationship with all men

And thus, I do not subject myself to any invisible man.

For if a man does not know he is a man,

How can he treat someone else with dignity and respect?

Questions to My Lover

After loving the people you send me,

Who is left for me?

Am I to be alone?

Where does a giver go for love?

Have I no home, no place to call my own.

What existence have I,

And sometimes it is not as wonderful as apple pie.

Lord, I need you.

I will take no hostages for my journey,

But you...you promised.

Am I trapped in the promise of love?

Wanting but not having, seeking but not finding.

Knocking, with no open door

I thought I was the one you adored.

Am I blue because it is true,

Or am I blue because of you?

How much do you love me?

How much do you want me?

Love paid the sacrifice once,

But I feel like I have paid it twice.

Maybe I am not being nice…

Can I suffice?

What is real and what is not?

Am I the affection of your love?

Lord, I need you, and I need you now.

Will I ever be satisfied?

I am thirsty but

I have no water for my thirst.

Are you expecting me to rise to the occasion

Like "the Phoenician woman"? (the Phoenician woman in the bible)

I have no strength for the journey.

Will you send for me?

Ready or not

Will you love me?

Will you quench the longing thirst of my heart?

Have I delighted myself in you?

Is it possible for me to please you?

Is my faith as small as a mustard seed?

Or is my faith gone with the wind?

Do I love you or am I pretending to love you?

How long must we endure the masquerade?

I am your lover.

While I play with you, I am not hiding from you.

Pursue me and take me over.

Am I too playful?

What's wrong with wanting to be caught by you?

I love lying in your arms.

Your chest...your everything…

Must I ask, where are you now?

I need you beside me.

Learning to Love...

"THE MIND DEFINES, DECIDES, DOUBTS AND DIVIDES -
ONLY THE HEART TRULY BINDS."

RASHEED OGUNLARU

The Road to You

The road to you makes me feel blue.

It reminds me of you,

The you that I do not have…

The you that I use in my mind to pass time…

The you that I use to avoid living this life.

It is easier loving someone else instead of loving myself.

The road to you encompasses all that I yearn for.

How could Pat Metheny have read my heart?

Could he have been led by the Spirit

To embrace my most intimate cares

And dares of this thing

We call "life"?

So mellow, full of sweetness,

His sound permeates my heart.

Or could it be that

My heart echoed so loudly that God above

Opened Pat Metheny's spiritual ear to hear my cry?

Maybe he heard it before I

cried…mmm.

The road to you

Could be what the ocean sounds like

if it spoke in melodious terms.

I once saw the Mediterranean Sea.

It was a deep, magnificent blue.

A blue that reminds me of your song that is

now etched on the circumference of my heart.

If my being was music instead of flesh,

The road to you is what it would sound like.

Silky, fiery red satin, with hues of tangerine in

The backdrop of a blazing sunset floating

Majestically over the waves of

Melodiousness in harmonic rhythm.

Black Velvet

Dark as the night

His skin is smooth like *black velvet*.

Liquid candy apple oozing from his pores,

He is a silhouette of perfection

In the backdrop of the moonlight.

His shadow illuminates the room.

His skin beckoned my touch.

Caressed by my eyes, engulfed my spirit,

I soaked up his loveliness into my being.

His skin quivers, anticipating a massage from my lips.

They became full by the rush of blood

From my vessels.

The sheer excitement of knowing that we are one

Causes my tissues and cells to

Exclaim your gentle dominance over my vesture.

My vesture is a mango skinned delight with a

Brush of Arizona red soil.

With the sweetness of pineapple which seeps out like nectar,

I welcomed you into a space created by our love.

A space unknown to me before,

A space I did not know existed,

A space created by our harmony,

Of wanting to know each other biblically.

Beyond the rim of knowing each other emotionally,

We wanted to inhabit each other.

The Count Who Loved Me

Incapacitated by my fascination with you,

I abandoned myself.

Texting by day and talking by night,

Consumed by the possibilities,

Permeated by spoken and unspoken words, we danced

A magnificent dance.

Filled with the colors of the wind I abandoned myself.

Burnt orange, vibrant yellow, and hues of brown.

We danced in concert,

Exchanging the depths of open hearts filled with glee.

It was magical.

We were spell-bound with words.

Not ordinary words, but words that entwined us,

Words that undressed us emotionally,

And confessed us spiritually.

As we twirled round and round,

You unwound us.

Suddenly without notice,

I felt ill at ease with you.

Bitten by your draconian tactics,

I fell into a trance where I heard you say,

"I love you too much to condemn you to a life

Flavored with a bit of darkness."

I had no idea who you were or what you were capable of.

You spoke of your weaknesses,

And I passed no judgment upon you.

I was willing to sacrifice His principals

For a little piece of your heaven.

Abandoned by you, I fell into His arms,

The One who loves me.

Finally, I saw that my lover took over the dance,

As He said, "Excuse me, I'll lead."

I Was Near Death

I was near death when he awakened me.

He spoke to my heart and ministered to my soul,

While never physically touching me.

"Arise," he cried.

I awakened to the most splendid love.

He caressed my wounds.

He dried my eyes with his gentle, sweet lips.

He kissed my forehead ever so kindly.

He kissed each tear, not allowing one to escape.

The aroma of his breath was warm,

Like apple cider on a brisk winter day.

Clean, crisp, fresh, and clear.

I could not defend myself against the passion I felt.

I was enchanted by the mere thought of touching your earlobe.

It looked soft and succulent.

My mouth watered for the opportunity.

My feet moved hastily toward you

Yet, I was standing still.

And then it came…

I was asked to summon you from sleep.

I was frozen in a funereal-like trance.

I visualized myself under the light of the candle

Reaching out to your earlobe.

It beckoned me.

I danced around with the thought of

Possessing it all night.

I wondered if I could really do it…

I could say,

"Oops…I am sorry, I accidentally touched you."

Under the shadow of the candle,

I reached out ever so gingerly several times that

Night to touch your earlobe,

but I acquiesced.

Random Thoughts on the Journey Towards Healing...

"AND THE LORD WENT BEFORE THEM BY DAY IN A PILLAR OF CLOUD TO LEAD THEM ALONG THE WAY, AND BY NIGHT IN A PILLAR OF FIRE TO GIVE THEM LIGHT, THAT THEY MIGHT TRAVEL BY DAY AND BY NIGHT."

EX 13:21 ESV

Too Tired to Pray

Are we too tired to pray

Amidst the haywire of decay?

Help us today, not to stray too far away.

Living on the run

Trying to have some fun

Trying to pay the bills, while soothing

The ills of this life

That sometimes cut you like a knife.

Didn't see it coming

When I was a youngin'.

Now I'm living pay to pay

Day by day, just trying to find my way.

I used to work two jobs, but I sobbed

When I saw them chil'en left alone

With no daddy at home

No one to call their own.

I moaned and I groaned, and I sang a sad song

That belonged to those who bear my pain

Upon the glass they stain.

On the bus or train,

We ride to and from trying to make ends meet

Trying to avoid defeat.

We miss it by a beat

And now I must retreat!

Spiritual Constipation

The congregation sits in anticipation

Of another sermon.

Happily, they meet and greet each week

Suffering from *Spiritual Constipation*.

Permeated through stagnation,

They sit in the pews

Feeling as if they have paid their dues.

They have retired

From their initial desire

To lead folks to Christ.

"Let someone else do the work!'

They say while they sit and watch at bay.

Chosen

Chosen to heal

Chosen to reveal

Chosen to do *His* will

Chosen to pray

Chosen to obey

Chosen to hear

Chosen to bare

Chosen to dare

Chosen to repair

Those with lots of despair

Chosen not to kill

Chosen to rebuild

The Courage to Live

I can't say I have the courage to live.

While He gives and gives,

I falter at the altar.

Over and over again, I struggle to win…

The battle that rages within!

Bankrupt

I have squandered my emotions,

Misused trust,

Ransacked voids and emptiness,

Filled them with anything I could find

With no regard to the cost or combination.

Clothes, shoes, handbags,

Pecans, dried fruit, bread, sugar,

And yet I cry.

With all of that,

I accuse myself of misappropriation of

"My temple."

I stole from myself.

Who is left to fill "my temple?"

And yet I cry for lack.

My bills are filled to the brim,

My girls are filled with ambition.

They want an education.

I wish I could assist but

My barrel is empty…

BANKRUPT.

Interruption of Everything

I thought she would never die.

I thought she would go on living and living.

I thought she would live into oblivion

Like at a wedding when the pastor asks,

"Who will give this lady in marriage?"

I thought our love and bond

Would never be broken.

And then it came...

The interruption of everything.

Her sweet smile, her laughter,

Her kindness, her intuitiveness,

And like at a wedding, everyone came to show their

Love and support.

They offered soothing words and acts of kindness.

They were there for me

And after the dust settled, I was standing there alone.

Sugar

The whites keep calling me.

Even though I know I should flee,

I embrace them with jubilee.

They are my enemy!

White rice that makes me feel nice

Especially when it's diced with spice.

And then there is white bread

That makes my colon dead.

Can't get a good move

When I delight in its groove.

I can deal with the dead bread that makes me

Mixed up in the head.

A little dizziness ain't nothing compared to

The business of that sweet stuff called sugar.

Aw, my sweet sugar…

Sometimes I am strong

And I think nothing can go wrong.

I start singing a new song

Where I know I belong.

Whole grains, fruits, nuts, and vegetables

And I's a be doing just fine.

For quite some time and like a thief in the night,

I am in a fight

Trying to ignore the "white call" who

Encourages me to fall.

Always dressed to kill

Sporting pastries and different kinds of niceties

Willing to please and ease my every

Ache and pain.

In vain I give in to my meager whim

Because I don't want to abandon them.

Well, I do...but I don't.

I know the whites are no good for me,

But when I get tired of relying on my Maker and

My King, then my emptiness makes me sing.

And my sweet sugar calls and says,

"You rang?"

No strength to say, "no!"

I just simply go, without a fight, or a prayer

To the one who would willingly be my slayer

Of every negative vice,

That could possibly leave me cold as ice.

New Beginnings...

"BEHOLD, I AM DOING A NEW THING; NOW IT
SPRINGS FORTH, DO YOU NOT PERCEIVE IT? I WILL
MAKE A WAY IN THE WILDERNESS AND RIVERS IN
THE DESERT."

ISAIAH 43:19 ESV

He Peeled Away Layers of my Heart

He peeled back the layers of my heart.

It was so well protected and my tightly kept secret was safe.

I laughed, played, and danced but I had never given

Myself to another.

Oh! It seemed so but it was not true.

From the moment we began to take walks I knew that I

Was experiencing an admiration for

Someone else who reminded me of God.

He had a kindness that was rare.

I was disarmed.

When we parted, I felt like we would

Never be separated spiritually.

When I left him,

He gave me the embrace of a lifetime.

His broad chest and masculine arms engulfed me.

I was swallowed up.

For that moment, time stood still.

I felt the words of his heart

Please never leave me.

But I had to go.

As time went by, we spoke and wrote.

Little by little I began to emerge into the real me,

The me I had never known.

I wanted to put everything back into that place of safety,

But his love weakened and strengthened me

All at the same time.

I begged and pleaded to not be released,

But without my knowledge, it happened…

Layer by layer,

Like the petals of a flower

The petals of my vesture became free.

My beauty had emerged

Without him taking the sweetness that lied within.

After a while, I could not bear the pain of not seeing him.

What happened next I was not prepared for…

What he did in my absence he now gave me.

He bathed me.

I wondered, *how could he?*

For he had never loved before, he soaped me up.

He bathed every crevice. He made me feel wanted,

beautiful, desired.

Was it real? Can I go back? I wondered

I wanted to pack up my petals, put them back

in my heart and take my leave.

Can one retrieve petals from the wind?

Where would I go? How could I leave?

His love overpowered me.

As I lie in his bed, he asked for my permission before

He touched me.

All of my members rejoiced as my blood rushed.

His kiss was gentle and he took his time.

Like the maestro on his instrument

Who goes from one end of the piano to the other

Without missing a beat.

The maestro who makes love to the notes ever so gently,

Strokes the keys with love,

A love that is communicated

With every touch and sound.

It is reverberated throughout his tune

And as the audience hears it,

They are suspended in mid air

As he rises to the crescendo.

Will I?

Will I be pardoned for my sins?

Who will mend my horrible bend

Of sin that I fight to win?

I surrender my will in order to fulfill

His highest desire to inspire.

Made in the USA
Middletown, DE
07 November 2022